DATE DUE		

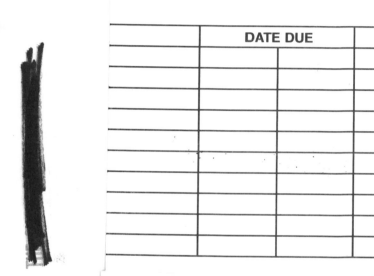

RARE ANIMALS

A CHAPTER BOOK

BY LINDA CASTERLINE

children's press®

A Division of Scholastic Inc.
New York Toronto London Auckland Sydney
Mexico City New Delhi Hong Kong
Danbury, Connecticut

For Aaron and Annmarie

"In wildness is the preservation of the world."
—Henry David Thoreau

ACKNOWLEDGMENTS

The author would like to thank all the dedicated people who work to save endangered animals from becoming extinct. In particular, she would like to thank the following people not only for their important work, but also for sharing their knowledge and giving their time to help make this book happen: Heather Ray of Operation Migration; Daphne and Angela Sheldrick of the David Sheldrick Wildlife Trust; Greg Marshall, executive producer and director of remote imaging for National Geographic Television and Film; and Richard Romaniuk, District Supervisor, Manitoba Conservation, Canada.

Casterline, Linda.
  Rare animals : a chapter book / by Linda Casterline.
    p. cm. – (True tales)
Summary: Introduces four endangered species–whooping cranes, elephants, monk seals, and polar bears–and describes what is being done to protect them and their habitats.
Includes bibliographical references and index.
  ISBN 0-516-22914-1 (lib. bdg.)   0-516-24607-0 (pbk.)
  1. Rare animals–Juvenile literature. 2. Endangered species–Juvenile literature. [1. Rare animals. 2. Endangered species. 3. Wildlife conservation.] I. Title. II. Series.
  QL83.C27 2003
  591.68–dc21
                        2003003914

1 2 3 4 5 6 7 8 9 10 R 12 11 10 09 08 07 06 05 04 03

CONTENTS

INTRODUCTION

A whooping crane looks for frogs in the marsh. Elephants trumpet with joy when they meet up with their relatives. A Hawaiian monk seal and her pup splash in shallow water. A polar bear crouches on the ice, waiting for a seal.

These animals are not doing anything special. They are just living their lives. Yet they are in danger of becoming **extinct**.

Many people are trying to save these animals. Some are teaching whooping cranes how to **migrate** (MYE-grate). Others are caring for baby elephants that have lost their mothers. A video camera is being used to see what monk seals do while swimming in the ocean. Polar bears are put in a safe "jail" when they get too close to a town in Canada. Later, they are set free.

Here are some of their stories.

CHAPTER ONE

BORN TO FLY FREE

It was a clear and sunny morning on October 17, 2001. At a **wildlife refuge** (REF-yooj) in Wisconsin, a small **ultralight** airplane **taxied** (TAK-seed) down a runway. Seven whooping cranes ran behind it, flapping their wings. Soon they were up in the air. They were flying to Florida. Would they make it?

Sixty years ago, there were twenty-one whooping cranes in the world. Today, there are about 400. Many people have helped these beautiful birds **survive**. Some of them raise young birds and teach them how to migrate, or fly south, for the winter.

Young whooping cranes follow an ultralight airplane.

Whooping cranes are also called "whoopers." They are named for the loud sounds they make when they call each other. The calls can be heard 2 miles (3.2 kilometers) away!

Whooping cranes live in **wetlands**. Once the cranes lived all over central and eastern North America. Then people began to drain the wetlands. Hunters and farmers shot the cranes. Some people stole their eggs. By 1950, there was only one wild **flock** left.

In 1999, nine groups of people who work to help wildlife got together. They formed the Whooping Crane Eastern Partnership. The group planned to start a new flock of migrating cranes. First, they would hatch eggs from a **captive** flock. Then they would use ultralight airplanes to teach them to migrate.

In spring 2001, eleven eggs were picked to start the new flock. The eggs were put in an **incubator** (ING-kyuh-bay-tur) to keep them warm. Scientists (SYE-uhn-tiss) played recorded sounds to the eggs. One sound was a parent crane purring. The other sound was an ultralight plane.

At 5 feet (1.5 meters) tall, whooping cranes are the tallest birds in North America.

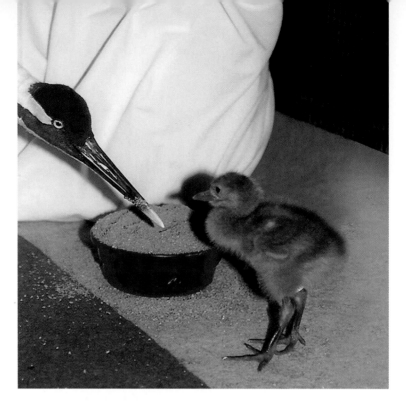

A puppet crane teaches a newly hatched chick how to eat.

When whooper chicks hatch, they **imprint** on whoever cares for them. The trainers did not want the cranes to think they were human. To fool the new chicks, the trainers used whooping crane costumes and puppets.

When the cranes were about eight weeks old, it was time for **flight** school. They learned to follow the ultralight plane down a grass runway. One by one they learned to fly. When the plane took off, the whoopers followed it into the air. The cranes went flying whenever the weather was good.

At last it was time to leave the wildlife refuge. Each crane had a tiny radio attached to one leg. This would help the trainers track them if they got lost. On the other leg was a colored band so the trainers could tell them apart. On October 17, eight whoopers followed an ultralight into the air. Two more planes followed the small flock.

An ultralight leads the young whoopers.

The young whoopers stretch their wings after a flight.

The group made many stops along the way. Often, the weather was too bad to fly. Sometimes the cranes would turn back. One crane had to be taken the rest of the way by truck. Once, the young birds would not fly across a busy highway. They were afraid of the trucks they could hear roaring below them. One crane flew into a power line and was killed.

The pilots and the rest of the cranes kept going. When they landed on December 3, everyone cheered. They had reached the whoopers' winter home in a Florida wildlife refuge. The cranes had flown 1,217 miles (1,959 kilometers). Their trip had taken forty-eight days.

In Florida, the seven whooping cranes lived on a small island. They ate snails, frogs, and crabs. Two of the cranes were killed by **bobcats**. Now there were five.

The cranes flew over bridges and busy highways.

Soon it was spring. Would the cranes go back to Wisconsin? Everyone waited to see. Finally, on April 9, 2002, the birds took off and headed north. This time, the cranes would fly by themselves. Would they be able to find their way back?

On April 19, four of the cranes landed in the refuge in Wisconsin. The birds had made the trip in only ten days! The fifth crane returned two weeks later. They had all made it! Whooping cranes were flying free in eastern North America for the first time in one hundred years.

CHAPTER TWO

CARING FOR BABY ELEPHANTS

A call comes in at the David Sheldrick Wildlife Trust, an elephant **orphanage** (OR-fuh-nij) in Kenya, Africa. A farmer has found a baby elephant trapped in a well. Its mother is gone. Workers, who are called keepers, go to the rescue. They bring the baby back to the orphanage where they will take care of it. When the elephant is old enough, it will be set free in a safe place.

Keepers rescue a baby elephant.

At one time, there were millions of elephants in Africa. Today, there are only about half a million left. Why? People have always hunted elephants for their tusks. Tusks are just two very long teeth, but they are made of ivory. Ivory is worth a lot of money. People carve it to make jewelry and works of art.

In the late 1900s, hunters came with new kinds of guns. They killed more and more elephants. People were afraid that all the elephants would be killed. Finally, new laws were made. Now, selling ivory is **illegal** (i-LEE-guhl) in most places. Fewer elephants are being killed for their tusks.

Today, elephants face another danger. Small farms dot the land where wild elephants once roamed. Hungry elephants eat crops. If the farmers can't scare the elephants away, they may shoot them. Most of the farmers are poor. If elephants eat their crops, they will go hungry. Yet the elephants are hungry, too. What can be done? Many people are working to find a way for the farmers and the elephants to share the land.

An elephant's tusks keep growing all its life.

Elephants and humans are alike in many ways. Elephants are smart and show signs of feeling happy, angry, or sad. They can live as many years as humans. Both live in close family groups. Baby elephants take as long to grow up as children do.

Baby elephants need their mother's milk for two years. If a baby elephant loses its mother, it will die. A mother may be killed for her tusks. She may be shot by farmers. A baby can fall into a well or get trapped in

A baby elephant drinks more than 9 quarts (8.5 liters) of milk every day.

A baby elephant plays with its keeper.

mud. The baby will be left behind if its family can't save it.

Daphne Sheldrick wanted to help these babies. She started the first elephant orphanage. She also figured out how to make a special kind of milk. An orphaned baby could drink it in place of its mother's milk. Now, people call Daphne when they find a baby elephant without its mother.

Once a baby elephant has been rescued, it is brought to the orphanage. An orphaned baby needs love, as

Daphne Sheldrick

A keeper sleeps with a baby elephant.

well as milk, to live. The keepers become
the baby's new family. They are always with
the baby elephants. They even sleep with
them at night.

When it is cool, elephants stand close
together to keep the babies warm. When it
is hot, an elephant mother will shade her
baby with her body. This helps keep the
baby from getting too hot. It also protects it
from getting sunburned. Keepers use a
blanket to keep an orphan warm. For shade,
they use big umbrellas. They rub the babies
with sunblock to protect their skin.

In the hottest part of the day, the keepers
take the babies for a mud bath. The babies

play in the red clay mud. The wet mud cools their skin and helps protect them from bug bites. The mud makes their gray skin look reddish-brown.

When the babies are about a year old, they leave the orphanage. They ride in trucks that take them to Tsavo East National Park. The keepers go, too. At the park, the baby elephants will stay in a fenced pen at night. There they will be safe from lions and other **predators** (PRED-uh-turs).

Elephants taking a mud bath

During the day, the orphans will go out into the **bush** with their keepers. There they will find plants to eat. They will take mud baths in a waterhole. The keepers still give the babies milk to drink as well as water.

Older orphans that now roam free may stop by for a visit. The babies **bond** with older female orphans. These elephants will help young orphans learn about life in the wild. When the orphans are old enough, they will leave the pen. They will form their own **herd** or join a wild one. They will be free, back in the wild where they belong.

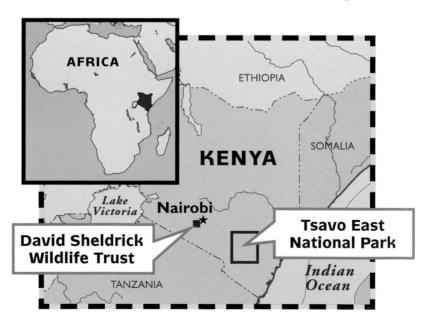

AFRICA

ETHIOPIA

SOMALIA

KENYA

Lake Victoria

Nairobi

David Sheldrick Wildlife Trust

Tsavo East National Park

TANZANIA

Indian Ocean

CHAPTER THREE

TRACKING SEALS UNDERWATER

A Hawaiian monk seal waddles down the beach and flops into the water. Where will it go? What will it eat? A video camera called a **Crittercam** is attached to the seal's back. Maybe the camera would help scientists answer these questions.

In the last fifteen years, scientists have learned a lot about the monk seal. How did they do it? They used **high-tech** (HYE-tek) tools to track the seals in the ocean. Some seals were fitted with radio sets

that send signals to **satellites** (SAT-uh-lites).
Then signals were sent back to scientists on
Earth. Other seals wore video cameras.
Later, scientists could look at the videos and
see what the seals did underwater.

A Hawaiian monk seal and her pup

Monk seals live in the tiny northwest islands of Hawaii. There are fewer than 1,400 Hawaiian monk seals left alive.

A female monk seal gives birth to one pup every two years. Her rich milk helps the pup grow fat. In about six weeks, it gains up to 170 pounds (77 kilograms). The mother doesn't eat during this time. She may lose as many pounds as the pup gains. When her body stops making milk, she goes away. After that, the pup is on its own. It must learn to find food for itself.

Monk seals eat fish, octopuses, lobster, and other small animals. Yet no one knew

A Hawaiian monk seal resting on a beach

how far they went to find food until the
Crittercam was invented.

In 1986, Greg Marshall saw a shark swim
by. A small fish was attached to its skin.
Greg had an idea. Why not attach a video
camera to a shark? Wouldn't that be a great
way to see what it did underwater? It would
be like looking through the shark's own
eyes. He called the camera Crittercam.

Since then, the Crittercam has been used to study many animals. One is the monk seal. On some islands, young monk seals are dying. It seems they may not be getting enough to eat. Is it because they can't find food? Maybe, but no one knows much about how or where monk seals look for food.

Crittercams were attached to more than twenty seals. Scientists had thought the seals hunted close to shore. They were in for a big surprise. The seals swam far out to sea. They hunted in water more than 200 feet (61 meters) deep. Later, scientists learned that some seals dive as deep as 1,500 feet (457 meters). There the seals swim along the ocean floor looking for food. Why couldn't they find enough?

Greg Marshall

Scientists come up to a seal wearing a Crittercam.

Scientists thought there was less food for the seals to find than there had been before. Some said it was because of changes in the **climate** (KLYE-mit). Others said it was because of the **fisheries**. The boats were catching too many lobsters and fish. There weren't enough left for the seals. Both reasons may be true.

What's most important is to protect the seals' feeding grounds. In December 2000,

President Bill Clinton signed an order to do just that. The ocean around all the northwest Hawaiian Islands is now a **nature reserve**. No one can drill for oil or gas. No one can dump trash. No one can catch too many fish.

Now there is hope for the Hawaiian monk seal. Maybe, someday, it will no longer be in danger of becoming extinct.

CHAPTER FOUR

TRAVELERS OF
THE ARCTIC

It is fall in Churchill, a small town in northern Canada. Nearby, a mother polar bear and her cubs are looking for something to eat. Suddenly, they smell something.

What could it be? The hungry bears follow the smell to the town dump. Garbage! Maybe they can find some food.

A few people are dropping off their trash. They see the polar bears and run away. Will the bears chase them? No. They are too busy looking for food. Still, the people are scared. They don't want the polar bears in their town. Why are the bears there? Why aren't they hunting for seals?

A mother polar bear with her cubs

Polar bears live in the Arctic, the area around the North Pole. The Arctic is one of the coldest places on Earth. Some of the Arctic is frozen land, but most of it is ocean. Ice covers this ocean much of the year.

The Inuit, people who live in the Arctic, have always hunted polar bears. They killed the bears for their meat, blubber, and fur. Still, they never killed too many. Then, in the 1950s, hunters came from many lands. They shot the bears from airplanes. Soon, there were only about 5,000 polar bears.

Many people wanted to save the polar bears. They worked together in all the Arctic countries. Laws were passed to stop the hunting. The laws worked. Fewer bears were killed. More bear cubs grew up safely. Today, there are up to 40,000 polar bears.

Every fall, lots of polar bears gather on the shore of Hudson Bay near Churchill.

They have gathered there for hundreds of years. The bears are waiting for the ice to freeze. Then they can go out on the ice to hunt for seals.

Thick fur and a layer of fat called blubber keep polar bears warm. To cool off, a polar bear stretches out on the ice.

Adult male bears mostly stayed away from Churchill. Female polar bears were more likely to wander into town with their cubs. The mothers had not had much to eat for six to eight months. Sometimes the bears took food from houses. People were afraid of them.

The garbage dumps were the polar bears' favorite places. The hungry bears ate the garbage. They made a mess. People wanted the bears to leave the dumps alone. They wanted the bears to stay out of town, too. At first, they shot at the bears to make them go away. Some bears were killed.

Some people in Churchill wanted to help the bears. The dump closest to town was closed. The main dump was fenced in. Also, people set special traps that catch bears, but don't hurt them. People put the traps near the dump and the roads.

A cub pokes its head through a kitchen window.

Hungry polar bears look for food
in a Churchill garbage dump.

The traps work well. Whenever a bear gets caught, it goes to a special "jail" for polar bears. If the jail fills up, the bears inside are moved to another place. Then there's room for more bears. About two or three dozen bears go to jail every year. When Hudson Bay freezes, the bears in the jail are let out on the ice. They are free to hunt for seals on the frozen bay.

A polar bear "jail"

This Polar Bear Alert program also teaches people how to watch out for bears. If you see a bear in Churchill, you can call the Polar Bear Alert line. Then the wildlife police will come and take the bear to jail.

A Polar Bear Alert sign near Churchill

Now, polar bears face new dangers. One is drilling for oil in the Arctic. Oil spills can hurt polar bears and the seals they eat.

The biggest danger is **global warming**. Earth has been getting warmer for the last hundred years. If this keeps up, the Arctic winter will get shorter. Polar bears do most of their hunting in the winter. If they only have a short time to hunt, they may not get enough to eat.

The polar bears near Churchill already have less time to hunt. They have lost two weeks of hunting in the fall and two weeks in the spring.

Today, scientists are looking for new ways to help polar bears. We can only hope that their work will pay off. Then the great white bears can go on roaming free in their land of ice and snow.

GLOSSARY

bobcat a small North American wildcat with a short tail

bond become close to

bush a wild place where few people live

captive not wild

climate (KLYE-mit) the normal weather of a place over a period of time

Crittercam a remote video camera that can be attached to an animal to record its comings and goings

extinct gone forever

fishery a company whose workers catch fish to be sold for food

flight the act of flying

flock a group of birds

global warming the heating up of Earth's climate due to waste from human activities

herd a large group of animals

high-tech (HYE-tek) (short for high technology) modern electronics and computers

illegal (i-LEE-guhl) against the law

imprint to learn by watching what another does

incubator (ING-kyuh-bay-tur) a machine that keeps eggs warm

migrate (MYE-grate) to move from one area to another

nature reserve a place where nature is left undisturbed

orphanage (OR-fuh-nij) a place where animals without mothers are cared for

predator (PRED-uh-tur) an animal that hunts other animals for food

satellite (SAT-uh-lite) a machine that orbits Earth

survive to stay alive

taxi (TAK-see) to drive an airplane along the ground

ultralight a very light one-person airplane with a small motor

wetlands places where the ground is very wet, such as a marsh or a swamp

wildlife refuge (REF-yooj) a place where people manage the land for animals

FIND OUT MORE

Born to Fly Free
www.operationmigration.org
Get up-to-date information on the whooping crane migration project.

www.savingcranes.org/kids/default.asp
To learn more about whooping cranes, click on the eggs at the top of the page.

Caring for Baby Elephants
www.sheldrickwildlifetrust.org
After you read the latest news about the orphans, watch their video.

www.globiokids.org
Follow an orphaned elephant as it is prepared to be returned to the wild.

Tracking Seals Underwater
www.nationalgeographic.com/crittercam/frameset.html
Click on pictures of animals and learn how Crittercam works on them. You can also watch a video of what a seal sees underwater.

Travelers of the Arctic
www.polarbearsalive.org
Learn how people help polar bears.

More Books to Read

African Elephants by Roland Smith, Lerner Publishing Group, 1995

And Then There Was One: The Mysteries of Extinction by Marjorie Facklam, Sierra Club Books, 1993

North American Cranes by Lesley A. DuTemple, Lerner Publishing Group, 1999

Polar Bears by Dorothy H. Patent, Carolrhoda Books, 2000

INDEX

PHOTO CREDITS

MEET THE AUTHOR

Linda Casterline was born in Pennsylvania. She has one grown-up son of whom she is very proud. She currently lives with her cat, Josephine, just outside New York City. Linda has worked as a children's book editor for many years. She likes reading, going for long walks, and watching birds and other wild animals.

Today, more than forty kinds of animals become extinct every day. Why? Mostly because of things people do. Take driving. Big cars burn lots of gas. Getting more gas could one day mean drilling for oil in the Arctic, where polar bears live. Shipping oil burns even more fuel and could cause an oil spill. Burning gas releases chemicals into the air that help cause global warming. So when you grow up, think carefully about what you do and how it may affect the other creatures of Earth.